ON THE CASE!

FIRE INVESTIGATORS

Madison Capitano

Rourke
Educational Media

A Division of
Carson Dellosa Education

Before Reading: *Building Background Knowledge and Vocabulary*

Building background knowledge can help children process new information and build upon what they already know. Before reading a book, it is important to tap into what children already know about the topic. This will help them develop their vocabulary and increase their reading comprehension.

Questions and Activities to Build Background Knowledge:

1. Look at the front cover of the book and read the title. What do you think this book will be about?
2. What do you already know about this topic?
3. Take a book walk and skim the pages. Look at the table of contents, photographs, captions, and bold words. Did these text features give you any information or predictions about what you will read in this book?

Vocabulary: *Vocabulary Is Key to Reading Comprehension*

Use the following directions to prompt a conversation about each word.

- Read the vocabulary words.
- What comes to mind when you see each word?
- What do you think each word means?

> **Vocabulary Words:**
> - *ammonium nitratre*
> - *arson*
> - *burn patterns*
> - *hazardous*
> - *hypothesis*
> - *origin*

During Reading: *Reading for Meaning and Understanding*

To achieve deep comprehension of a book, children are encouraged to use close reading strategies. During reading, it is important to have children stop and make connections. These connections result in deeper analysis and understanding of a book.

Close Reading a Text

During reading, have children stop and talk about the following:

- Any confusing parts
- Any unknown words
- Text to text, text to self, text to world connections
- The main idea in each chapter or heading

Encourage children to use context clues to determine the meaning of any unknown words. These strategies will help children learn to analyze the text more thoroughly as they read.

When you are finished reading this book, turn to the next-to-last page for **After Reading Questions** and an **Activity**.

TABLE OF CONTENTS

ON THE CASE

Some fire investigators start as firefighters. Some begin as scientists. They can specialize in chemistry, computer science, **hazardous** materials, and more. All of them work hard to solve the mysteries fires can leave behind.

» **hazardous** (HAZ-ur-duhs): dangerous or risky

4

Investigators used to rely on personal experiences or well-known myths instead of scientific evidence. But in the last 50 years, there have been huge advancements in fire science! Investigators work hard to bust myths and provide better answers about why fires start.

HEATING UP COLD CASES

In 1970, a 16-year-old boy was convicted of arson and murder. Police pointed to matches in the boy's pocket and other evidence. In 2010, fire investigators looked at the case with new technology. They concluded it was an accidental fire, not arson.

» **arson** (AHR-suhn): the crime of setting fire to property with willful or malicious intent

7

A TINY SPARK

A sudden forest fire has firefighters working hard! But what caused it?

Don't worry; the fire investigators are on the case.

To solve the mystery, fire investigators use the scientific method. They observe. They ask questions. They form a **hypothesis** and make a prediction. Then, they perform tests to see if they are right!

» **hypothesis** (hye-PAH-thi-sis): an idea that could explain something, but that has to be tested or proven true

11

Investigators also try to find where the fire began. They look for the area of **origin** and the point of origin. The area of origin can be big. The point of origin is often small.

In this case, the point of origin was a campfire that was not put out properly! A tiny spark can cause a big fire.

» **origin** (OR-i-jin): the point where something starts, or the cause of something

12

WHAT GETS LEFT BEHIND

A house fire broke out last night! Some think it was an accident. But was it? Detectives need answers, and the fire investigator is on the case!

There are ways a fire investigator can tell if a fire was set using accelerants. Accelerants are substances often used in arsons to make fires spread faster. Investigators ask questions to find out how fast a fire burned. They look for **burn patterns** that accelerants leave behind.

» **burn patterns** (burn PAT-urns): the visible, measurable physical changes or identifiable shapes formed by a fire

17

Certain accelerants can also change the color or smell of fires. When a fire investigator suspects arson, they take samples from the point of origin and send them to a lab. The lab will test for common accelerants such as gasoline, diesel fuel, and acetone.

DIFFERENT CLUES

Depending on what is in the fire, investigators see or smell different things. Fires with magnesium produce a very bright light. Accelerants such as gasoline leave a smell. Rubbing alcohol produces a blue flame.

MAGNESIUM FIRE

18

CHEMICAL FIRE

WOOD FIRE

19

Witnesses say that the fire spread quickly and that the smoke was black. The fire investigator sees suspicious burn patterns. They discover the point of origin in a bedroom and collect samples for the lab. All the evidence shows this was a gasoline fire!

The fire investigator tells the police it was definitely arson.

TESTING 1, 2, 3

When investigators collect evidence, they must leave enough room in the bag for gases to gather. This gas is what labs examine!

21

AN EXPLOSIVE MYSTERY

A trailer explodes, and no one knows why. Police need to know if they should be looking for suspects. A fire investigator is on the case!

Fire investigators also investigate explosions. Some explosions are the result of arson. Other explosions can happen if an accidental fire reaches explosive or hazardous material.

LEARNING BY DOING

Fire investigators experiment with explosions and fires in controlled environments. They measure things like the heat of the fire, the time it takes to burn, and the burn patterns left behind. They use this information to better investigate fires.

This trailer had bags of fertilizer in it. The fertilizer contained **ammonium nitrate**. This compound helps plants grow, but it is also an explosive chemical. The investigator found that an accidental cooking fire caused the fertilizer to burn. Then, the trailer exploded!

» **ammonium nitrate** (uh-MOH-nee-uhm NYE-trayt): a white crystalline salt that is used as a fertilizer and as a component of some explosives, NH_4NO_3

26

Fire investigators work hard to apply science to fires and explosions. They use technology and investigative skills to help police understand the evidence that fires leave behind. Fire investigators are on the case!

MEMORY GAME

Look at the pictures. What do you remember
reading on the pages where each image appeared?

INDEX

AFTER READING QUESTIONS

1. What does *arson* mean?

2. What do fire investigators look for?

3. What is the difference between a point of origin and an area of origin?

4. What clues can mean a fire was set on purpose?

5. What is *ammonium nitrate* used for?

ACTIVITY

Some fires smell different if an accelerant is used. Put your nose to the test! Gather things around your house that have a strong smell, such as spices and unlit candles. Now, close your eyes. Have a friend or parent hold each item up. See if you can identify the smells without looking.

ABOUT THE AUTHOR

Madison Capitano is a writer in Columbus, Ohio, who loves to have campfires with her friends! But they always make sure to put them out properly. Madison used to read books to her little brother and sister all the time. Now she loves to write books for other kids to enjoy.

© 2021 Rourke Educational Media

All rights reserved. No part of this book may be reproduced or utilized in any form or by any means, electronic or mechanical including photocopying, recording, or by any information storage and retrieval system without permission in writing from the publisher.

www.rourkeeducationalmedia.com

PHOTO CREDITS: page 1: ©TK / Shutterstock; page 5: ©VAKS-Stock Agency / Shutterstock; page 6: ©Scott Leman / Wikimedia; page 9: ©MarginalCost / Shutterstock; page 10: ©Kulchan S / Shutterstock; page 13: ©erikjohnphotography / Shutterstock; page 15: ©katacarix / Shutterstock; page 16: ©Lukasz Sadlowski / Shutterstock; page 19: ©VAKS-Stock Agency / Wikimedia; page 19: ©Capt. John Yossarian / iStockphoto; page 19: ©Pgiam / Shutterstock; page 20: ©k_samurkas / Newscom; page 23: ©Glen Stubbe / Shutterstock; page 24: ©TFoxFoto / Shutterstock; page 27: ©Lukasz Sadlowski / Shutterstock; page 28: ©Srinuan hirunwat / iStockphoto; caution tape: ©vm / Pixabay; magnifying glass: ©tcenitelkrasoti / Pixabay

Edited by: Kim Thompson
Cover design by: Kathy Walsh
Interior design by: Sara Radka

Library of Congress PCN Data

Fire Investigators / Madison Capitano
(On the Case!)
    ISBN 978-1-73163-816-8 (hard cover)
    ISBN 978-1-73163-893-9 (soft cover)
    ISBN 978-1-73163-970-7 (e-Book)
    ISBN 978-1-73164-047-5 (e-Pub)
Library of Congress Control Number: 2020930177

Rourke Educational Media
Printed in the United States of America
01-1942011937